I didn't know that

WORLD OF WONDER
WOW
WORLD OF WONDER

Get ready to hear your kids say, "Wow! I didn't know that!" as they dive into this fun, informative, question-answering series of books! Students—and teachers and parents—will learn things about the world around them that they never knew before!

This approach to education seeks to promote an interest in learning by answering questions kids have always wondered about. When books answer questions that kids already want to know the answers to, kids love to read those books, fostering a love for reading and learning, the true keys to lifelong education.

Colorful graphics are labeled and explained to connect with visual learners, while in-depth explanations of each subject will connect with those who prefer reading or listening as their learning style.

This educational series makes learning fun through many levels of interaction. The in-depth information combined with fantastic illustrations promote learning and retention, while question and answer boxes reinforce the subject matter to promote higher order thinking.

Teachers and parents love this series because it engages young people, sparking an interest and desire in learning. It doesn't feel like work to learn about a new subject with books this interactive and interesting.

This set of books will be an addition to your home or classroom library that everyone will enjoy. And, before you know it, you, too, will be saying, "Wow! I didn't know that!"

"People cannot learn by having information pressed into their brains. Knowledge has to be sucked into the brain, not pushed in. First, one must create a state of mind that craves knowledge, interest, and wonder. You can teach only by creating an urge to know." - Victor Weisskopf

© 2012 Flowerpot Press

Contents under license from Aladdin Books Ltd.

Flowerpot Press
142 2nd Avenue North
Franklin, TN 37064

Flowerpot Press is a division of Kamalu, LLC,
Franklin, TN, U.S.A.,
and Mitso Media, Inc., Oakville, ON, Canada.

ISBN 978-1-77093-775-8

Concept, editorial, and design by
David West Children's Books

Designer:
Robert Perry

Illustrators:
Darren Harvey - Wildlife Art Ltd
Jo Moore

American Edition Editor:
Johannah Gilman Paiva

American Redesign:
Jonas Fearon Bell

Printed in China.

I didn't know that

sharks keep losing their teeth

I didn't know that

Introduction

Did you know that some sharks are older than dinosaurs? That most sharks are smaller than you? That some grow inside mermaid purses?

Discover for yourself amazing facts about sharks, like how big the whale shark is and how tiny the dwarf shark is. Find out what they eat, how they have babies, who their enemies are, and more.

 Watch for this symbol, which means there is a fun project for you to try.

 True or False? Watch for this symbol and try to answer the question before reading on for the answer.

Don't forget to check the borders for extra amazing facts.

I didn't know that

sharks are older than dinosaurs. Sharks' ancestors lived about 200 million years before dinosaurs. Some were giants and had spines on their head.

Can you find five trilobites?

Just a few sharks turned into fossils, but many of their teeth did! This tooth (left) measures almost 5 inches (12 centimeters) long, and belonged to a monster shark called "megalodon." A great white shark's tooth is half this size.

Cladoselache lived about 350 million years ago, and measured about 6.5 feet (2 meters) from teeth to tail. The shark's mouth was at the tip of its snout, not tucked underneath like most sharks today.

Cladoselache

This fossil of a shark called "stethacanthus" shows that it had thorny spines. Fossils of sharks are rare because their skeletons are made not of bone, but cartilage, which rots away before it can fossilize.

! Port Jackson sharks still have spines, just like their ancestors did.

I didn't know that

sharks are the biggest fish. The whale shark measures up to 42 feet (13 meters) long, and is the largest fish in the sea. This gentle giant feeds peacefully, filtering tiny plants and animals from the water.

Can you find three divers?

Whale shark

The dwarf shark is just 6 inches (15 centimeters) long, not much bigger than a goldfish. In fact, half of all known sharks measure less than 3 feet (1 meter) long.

Whale sharks are so gentle that divers can ride on them.

To see how big a whale shark really is, try making one in the park or on the beach. Using a yardstick (or meterstick) as a guide, measure out its length, then fill in the outline with pebbles or twigs.

The basking shark is the world's second largest fish. It swims with its mouth open to catch microscopic sea creatures.

Megamouth shark

I didn't know that

some sharks glow in the dark. Some sharks that live in the deep, dark parts of the ocean make their own light. The jaws of a megamouth shark give out a silvery glow. This probably helps attract tasty shrimp.

Can you find six jellyfish?

The frilled shark had elongated eyes to see in the murky depths.

The goblin shark (above) lives at the bottom of the sea. Its long, sensitive snout helps it find any nearby prey.

Sensitive snout

Lantern sharks (left) glow in the water, thanks to a shiny slime on their skin. Experts think the coloring may help sharks attract their prey or keep their place in a shoal.

The cookie-cutter shark gets its name from its curious bite. When the shark attacks another animal, it leaves a wound that is perfectly round—just like a cookie.

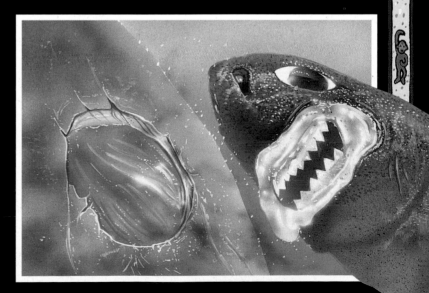

I didn't know that

some sharks have heads like hammers. The hammerhead shark has a "T" shaped head, just like the top of a hammer. As the shark swims, it swings its head from side to side so its eyes have an all-around view.

Great hammerhead shark

The wobbegong is a strange looking shark with speckled skin and tassels that make it look like a rock or seaweed. The fish makes use of this brilliant camouflage by hiding on the seabed and snapping up fish.

Stingray

Gill slits

Sharks are related to rays (left). Both groups of fish have gill slits instead of flaps, and skeletons of cartilage rather than bone.

 True or False?
Some sharks have wings.

Answer: **True**
The angel shark's large fins (right) are just like wings. It uses them to glide along the seabed as it searches for crustaceans and fish.

Angel sharks are called "monkfish" since they seem to be wearing a hood.

I didn't know that

if sharks stop swimming, they sink. Most fish have an air-filled bladder inside them, which helps keep them afloat in the sea. Sharks don't have swim bladders. To avoid sinking, most sharks have to swim all the time, like they are treading water.

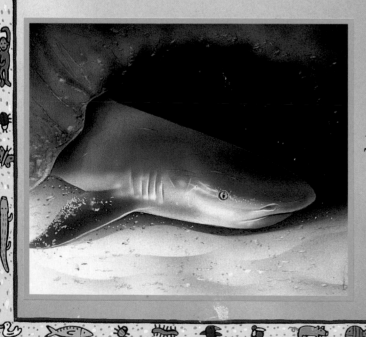

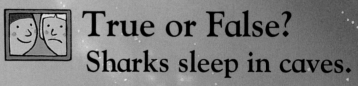 **True or False?**
Sharks sleep in caves.

Answer: **True**
The white-tip reef shark is a sleepy fish. At night, it cruises sluggishly around coral reefs, and spends the day sleeping on the seabed. It often hides away in caves to avoid being spotted and disturbed.

! The pectoral fins give a shark lift, just like the wings on a plane.

A shark's body is sleek, streamlined, and built for speed. Its fins are large and fairly stiff, and help it power forward, stay upright, steer, and stop.

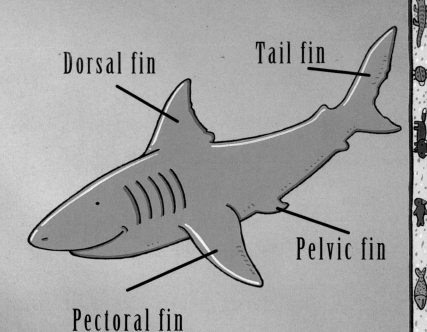

Dorsal fin

Tail fin

Pelvic fin

Pectoral fin

Mako shark

Like all fish, sharks have gills to take in oxygen from water. As water flows over the gills, tiny blood vessels absorb the oxygen and carry it around the body.

15

I didn't know that

sharks keep losing their teeth. Sharks often lose their teeth as they attack their prey, so new teeth constantly grow inside their mouths. Slowly, the new teeth form and move outwards to replace the older ones.

Can you find five teeth?

Sand tiger shark

A tiger shark has an enormous bite due to its ability to open its jaw so wide. The teeth have a sharp point and two serrated edges—perfect for seizing and slicing prey.

New teeth form

Older teeth will be replaced

Shark's teeth give clues to its diet. Most sharks have sharp, cutting teeth, but some have small files and filters to trap plankton, or blunt, broad teeth to crush shells.

Mako

Great white shark

Tiger shark

Whale shark

Nurse shark

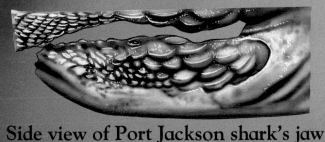

Side view of Port Jackson shark's jaw

Dogfish

Sharks can't chew their food. They have to swallow it in large chunks.

I didn't know that

sharks feed in a frenzy. When sharks feed, others may join in. As they snap at the food, they get excited by the blood and movement in the water. They can bite or kill each other during this "feeding frenzy."

A shark's jaw lies a long way under its pointed snout. As the fish lunges to bite, it lifts its nose out of the way, and swings its jaws forward. Then, it rolls up its eyes inside its head to protect them during the attack.

Sharks eat all kinds of foods: seabirds, seals, turtles, crustaceans, and plankton. They rarely eat people; they don't like the taste of human flesh!

Blue sharks

 True or False?
Some sharks attack with their tail.

Answer: **True**
The thresher shark has a long tail, which it lashes in the water like a whip. Scientists think that this either stuns its prey or herds fish into a tightly-knit group, which the thresher shark then attacks.

! ...an old tire, three raincoats, an anchor, and an oil drum.

I didn't know that

sharks can smell blood over a half mile (1 kilometer) away. Sharks have a keen sense of smell. As water streams past their nostrils, they pick up messages in the sea around them. When sharks sniff the blood of a wounded animal, they can power toward it.

Sharks have tiny organs on their snout that can pick up electrical signals. Since every creature in the sea produces some kind of electricity, these organs help sharks to hunt them down.

Shark skin was once used on sword handles to give a good grip.

Sharks have a lateral line on each side of their body, which picks up vibrations in the sea. It helps sharks to feel the things that are moving around them, such as a seal or a fish.

Can you find the other fish?

Oceanic white-tip shark

A shark's body is covered not with scales, but with tooth-like bumps called "denticles." These are very coarse, and feel rough if they're stroked the wrong way.

21

I didn't know that

some fish hitch rides on sharks. Remoras are small fish with a sucker pad on their head. They use it to cling onto sharks. As they ride, they help by eating parasites on the sharks.

Sucker pad

Can you find ten remoras?

Remoras ride on the waves made by sharks, just like they are surfing.

Zebra shark

Small, agile pilot fish often swim alongside a shark. They probably feel safe near their large companion, and can also feed on scraps of its food.

I didn't know that

some baby sharks grow inside leather purses. Some sharks lay their eggs in leathery cases called "mermaid purses." Inside the purse, the eggs grow into baby sharks. They eat the yolk and hatch 10 months later.

Can you find the mother shark?

Swell shark embryas

Seven months old

24

While some kinds of sharks hatch out of eggs, most develop inside their mother's body. They feed either on egg yolk or on food in their mother's blood, and are later born live, like mammals.

A baby lemon shark emerges from its mother.

Next time you're on the beach, try to find a mermaid's purse. The dogfish is a common shark, and its dry, black egg cases are often washed up on the shore.

Many sharks try to protect their eggs. The horn shark wedges her spiral-shaped egg case into a crack in a rock. Other egg cases have long tendrils that cling onto plants.

Horn shark egg

! A whale shark's egg is the size of a football.

I didn't know that

people are sharks' worst enemies. Large, meat-eating sharks have no enemies in the sea, but people kill them for sport, and for their meat, skin, and oil. Also, many sharks get trapped in fishing nets and drown.

Great white shark

True or False?
Sharks are blood-thirsty killers.

Answer: **False**
This is a myth that films, such as *Jaws* have helped to spread. Most sharks leave people alone. Scientists believe attacks only happen when a shark mistakes a swimmer for a seal or other kind of prey.

Seal

Surfer

Bull shark

Some people catch sharks for sport, and treat their bodies as trophies. Every year, the number of large sharks in the sea falls.

Sharks are killed so people can make soup from their fins, jewelry from their teeth, and medicines and lipsticks from their oil.

Shark liver oil pills

Shark fin soup

Jewelry

Cosmetics

Sharks seem to attack more men than women.

I didn't know that

shark scientists wear chain mail. Divers who study sharks need protection. Many wear chain mail suits called "neptunics," which are made from thousands of stainless steel rings. Sharks can't bite through the heavy suits.

Blue shark

Sonic tag

To study sharks, scientists need to be able to follow them. They do this by catching sharks, attaching sonic tags to their fins, and then returning them to the water. The tags give out radio signals, which the scientists carefully track.

Tiger shark

Tagging pole

Underwater photographers can safely film sharks from inside strong metal cages. It can still be a scary ordeal, though. Scientists attract the sharks with a strong-smelling bait. Sometimes the sharks crash heavily against the cage, trying to get inside!

Great white shark

The bubbles from a diver's aqualung scare some sharks.

Glossary

Bait
Food, such as a dead fish, which is used to attract sharks.

Camouflage
The colors and markings on an animal that help it to blend in with its surroundings.

Cartilage
The material that forms the skeletons of sharks and rays.

Crustacean
An animal, such as a lobster or a crab, that has a hard outer shell and lots of legs.

Fossil
Animal remains, which have turned to stone over millions of years.

Hibernate
To spend the winter in a kind of deep sleep.

Mammal
An animal, such as a cat, that gives birth to its young and feeds it on milk.

Organ
Any part of the body that has a special purpose, such as the eyes, which are the organs of sight, and the ears, which are the organs of hearing.

Parasite
An animal that lives on another animal (known as the host) and gets food from it. A parasite always damages its host.

Plankton
Microscopic plants and animals that live in the sea.

Ray
A kind of large, flat sea fish with wing-like fins and a long tail.

Serrated
Having a sharp, zig-zagging edge like a saw.

Streamlined
Having a smooth body shape that moves easily through the water.

Tapeworm
A long, flat worm that lives inside the stomach and intestines of other animals. It is a parasite.

Vibration
A shaking movement that is often felt rather than seen.

Yolk
The yellow part inside an egg, which provides food for the growing animal.

Index